Enter the Flow

Mindful Movement Qigong

By John Munro

Disclaimer

No part of this book is intended as medical advice, or to be used as a substitute for appropriate medical care.

Neither this nor any other exercise program should be followed without first consulting a health care professional. If you have any special conditions requiring attention, you should consult with your health care professional regarding the suitability of the exercises and practices contained in this book and possible modifications.

The author and publisher are not liable for any damage, injury or other adverse outcome resulting from the application of information contained in this book.

Copyright © 2017 John Munro

All rights reserved.

No part of this book may be reproduced in any form whatsoever, whether by graphic, visual, electronic, film, microfilm, tape recording, or any other means without prior written permission of the author, except in the case of brief passages embodied in critical reviews and articles.

ISBN-13:9781544805467

Printed by CreateSpace, An Amazon.com Company
Available from Amazon.com and other retail outlets

Foreword

In *Enter the Flow* our aim is to become aware of the energy flow throughout our bodies and to keep it flowing freely at all times.

Often when describing the movement of energy, water is used as an analogy to describe its flow or lack of it. Different qigong practices focus on different aspects of this flow. In the context of other practices, the *Enter the Flow* practice is like working with the clouds and rain. We are working with a general movement of energy that can go anywhere within our bodies, bringing fresh energy and vitality.

In a way this makes the *Enter the Flow* practices more simple than other qigong practices because we are not focusing on stimulating specific pathways and directions of flow. We are allowing the energy to flow in any direction and to any part of our body in a healthy way. This does present its own challenges though. Many of us find that we have many bad habits of posture, movement, and thought that can obstruct the flow of our energy. To begin with it may be difficult to feel the flow of energy at all, but as we become mindful of our movement and energy flow, little by little we can uncover and resolve these blockages.

With time and practice our aim is to maintain a healthy energy flow in our bodies at all times and in all situations. When we are successful at doing this we are truly 'in the flow'. Our every movement becomes more efficient and graceful. We are able to interact more skilfully with the world around us and we become less prone to strain or injury. Wherever the qi flows there is health and healing. As our qi flows more freely throughout our bodies we find that aches and pains go away, stiffness becomes supple, and areas of weakness in our body become strong.

Overtime every activity we engage in becomes more enjoyable. We find that there is pleasure in even the most mundane of tasks as we turn them into moving meditations where we are mindful of our movement and the sensations of our energy flow. There is joy in the experience of simply moving and being.

Because in *Enter the Flow* we are focusing on the free flow of energy within our bodies, the range of movements we can use in this practice is literally limitless. This book will present a variety of movements to help you to start to feel your flow of energy and develop healthy habits of energy flow within your movement, but once you have learned and practiced these you can and should apply these same principles to every type of movement. Because of this freedom of expression of the principles of energy flow, *Enter the Flow* practice can be a great source of creativity and inspiration in your life, and as you explore your energy flow in this way you can come to understand yourself and the world around you more fully.

At times you will find there is a bit of white space in this book. This has been inserted intentionally so that wherever possible the written instructions and photographs of each exercise can appear on facing pages to make it easier for you to follow. If you find that there are any of the exercises that you have difficulty understanding, you can find videos and other additional resources to help you on the Long White Cloud Qigong website, as well as information about other qigong practices you may be interested in. You can find further details about this in Chapter Ten: The Wide World of Qigong.

I hope that you enjoy the process of learning to feel and direct the healthy flow of energy within your body as you *Enter the Flow*!

Table of Contents

Disclaimer iii

Foreword v

Chapter One: The Flow State 1

   Preparation for Flow 3

      Allow Enough Time 3

      Clear Your Mind 4

      Centre Your Awareness In Your Body 5

      Breathe 5

      Repetition 5

      Slow Then Fast 6

Chapter Two: Playing With Waves 7

      Standing Posture 9

      Rise and Fall 10

      Rolling Waves – Forward and Back 13

      Lift Up Pour Down 16

Chapter Three: Empty and Full 18

      Side to Side 20

      Turning 22

      Forward and Back 24

      Walking 28

      Combinations 30

Chapter Four: Swimming Dragon 33

      Stir the Mist 34

      Swimming in the Mist 36

      Twist and Turn 38

Swimming Dragon	40
Chapter Five: Playing With A Ball	**43**
Forming a Ball	45
Holding a Ball	53
Lifting and Lowering	54
Holding to Each Side	56
Holding a Large Ball	58
Holding a Ball in One Hand	60
Bouncing and Throwing	62
Combinations	64
Chapter Six: Fighting Movements	**66**
Punching	68
Kicking	70
Blocking	72
Throwing	74
Shadow Fighting	76
Chapter Seven: Everyday Movements	**79**
Sweeping	81
Washing Dishes	82
Typing	83
Driving	84
Chapter Eight: Freestyle Qigong	**85**
Activating Your Energy	85
Ways to Work With The Energy Flow	86
Purposeful Practice	87
Creativity and Self Expression	88

    Healing Injury and Illness 89

    Specific Movement Refinement 90

    Energy Character Development 92

    More Abstract Purposes 93

Chapter Nine: Enter The Flow 95

Chapter Ten: The Wide World Of Qigong 99

About the Author 103

x

Chapter One: The Flow State

Was there ever a time that you were so absorbed in what you were doing that you lost all track of time? So focused that all other thoughts slipped away? Everything just seemed to work, you always knew what to do next, the pieces all just fell into place. There was a rhythm and flow to your every action, one following the other. The experience was so pleasurable that you could describe it as an altered state of consciousness, a state of incredible clarity, perhaps even ecstasy.

This incredible state of consciousness is experienced by artists, athletes, and musicians when they are totally focused on their activity and performing at their highest level. They become one pointed, present, and experience an immense sense of satisfaction in what they are doing.

In recent times this type of experience has become a popular subject of study in the field of positive psychology, and has come to be called being in a 'flow state' or 'in the zone'. It has been found that not only is this state associated with higher levels of performance, but how often someone achieves this state is a key determinant of their level of happiness and satisfaction with life.

This 'flow state' is not a new invention though, it has been experienced by people of all cultures throughout time, and the ancient traditions described this state and give us tools for how to achieve it.

Qigong is one such practice. Through heightened awareness of our body we clear all other thoughts from our mind and become fully immersed in the present moment and our present activity. One of the keys to this is learning to be aware not just of your physical body, but also the energy that flows through it. When we become aware of our energy we gain a much more nuanced sense of our activity. We are able to perceive many more aspects of what is happening physically than we would otherwise consciously be able to due to our limited capacity to process discrete pieces of information simultaneously.

Instead of focusing on each individual detail separately, when we tune in to our energy we become aware of the combined influence of each detail on the overall state and flow through our body. As we then work with this sense of energy flow in our body and adjust its quality, we then naturally adjust the corresponding details in our physical functioning.

To have healthy energy flow in your body, your joints need to be aligned so that physical forces transfer through the body efficiently. There must be neither too much nor too little tension in the muscles and connective tissues. There must be healthy blood flow and there must not be excessive pressure on any of the nerves. Rather than trying to address each of these factors separately; through relaxed concentration and awareness of the physical sensation in our body we adjust all of these at the same time to enhance our sense of energy flow.

When we tune in to this sense of energy flow in our bodies we are able to open the way for our body to heal itself, as the factors for healthy energy flow are the same factors that are required to heal and strengthen the body. All of our movements also become more efficient and graceful as we learn to use our body in healthier ways that preserve and protect it. Feeling healthy energy flow is also very pleasurable, so as we learn this skill we are able to take joy in even the simplest of tasks as we turn them into a gentle moving meditation.

We also quickly discover the role our mind has on the functioning of our body. We discover that thinking about things in different ways can lead to a completely different experience of the same activity. We start to uncover the connection between our mind and the tensions and patterns of activity in our body. Sometimes we cannot correct a pattern of movement and functioning in our body without first correcting the thoughts that are causing the pattern. With practice we become better at aligning our thoughts with our actions and desires to allow our energy to flow without restriction.

When we use mind and body in harmony in this way, we are truly in a flow state. Everything becomes easier as we find our way around and through blockages in our body and in our life.

This is not to say that entering a state of flow in this way is going to be easy. It is likely that to begin with you will find many blocks obstructing your flow. Perhaps so many that you can only catch a glimpse, a fleeting moment of energy awareness and flow as you begin your practice. But that is ok, as soon as you can find even a little awareness of energy flow within you, you can begin to work with it. Like water dripping on a rock, the energy will find a way around and eventually through even the most stubborn of blockages as you practice consistently, allowing your energy to flow free and unobstructed.

This book will teach you a variety of simple exercises and movements to start to become aware of your energy flow and to practice allowing it to flow more freely. Once you have developed awareness of energy in these simple movements we will look at how you can apply this same awareness to your everyday activities at home, at work, and at play.

Little by little energy flow will become a habit. This heightened awareness and sense of ease and satisfaction will become a natural way for you to be throughout your life rather than something you only achieve in moments.

Preparation for Flow

Here are a few suggestions for you to consider to prepare you for each of your Enter the Flow qigong practice sessions. These same principles will also apply as you begin to apply awareness of energy to the rest of your life.

Allow Enough Time

An important part of experiencing flow is to be fully present, to really experience the moment in detail. If you are in a rush, it implies that not all of your attention is on your present activity, some of it is on moving on to whatever you have to do next, hence the sense of rush takes away from your ability to experience the present moment. So before you start to practice you need to make sure that you have allowed yourself enough time to relax into the moment and experience it without thoughts about what is to come next. How much time you need to allow for your practice will depend on what you want to achieve in your session. To begin with it is a good idea to allow at least 15 minutes if you are going to focus on just one or two simple exercises. Of course you can practice for much longer if you want to, and particularly if you intend to practice more than a few exercises. When you are not experienced and skilled at entering a state of flow it takes time to ease yourself into it from your more habitual state of consciousness. With practice you will be able to do this more easily and quickly, and eventually it will become a habit that you can maintain throughout your day.

Clear Your Mind
During your practice session you want to focus on nothing else but your practice, so you will want to clear your mind of other thoughts. Sometimes to empty your mind you need somewhere to put what you empty out or it will just want to come back in again. Before you begin your practice session you can ask yourself if there is anything else you need to be thinking about or doing at that time. You can take a moment to take inventory of the thoughts that are in your mind. Unimportant ones can be set aside. Important thoughts you can decide if they are urgent or not. If they are truly urgent you may be better off attending to them rather than trying to practice qigong with them pressing on your mind. If they can wait for awhile, you can make a mental note of them so that you can come back to them when you have finished practicing, or you can go even further and make a physical note by writing them down if that helps you to clear your mind and leaves you more free to focus on the present moment during your qigong practice.

Centre Your Awareness In Your Body

Take a moment to tune in to your physical body. To feel the sensations of just being. If you like you can scan through your body bringing your awareness to every part and what you can feel in it. You can start with your feet and work your way up through your legs and then your torso and your arms, neck and head. When our thoughts are busy our attention goes to whatever we are thinking about and where ever that may be. We can quite literally lose awareness of our body and become 'disconnected'. In our qigong practice we want to become more connected on a deeper and deeper level. Taking a few moments to bring your awareness back into your body at the beginning of your session will help with this.

Breathe

Breathing is a great way to accomplish both of the previous two items. It is difficult to have a truly 'empty' mind when it is used to thinking a lot. It is far easier to give it something simply to focus on and achieve a relaxed and clear mind rather than an empty one. Focusing on the breath is an excellent way to do this as not only does the gentle rhythm of in an out give you something simple to focus on, it also helps you to be more aware of your body and the movement of force and energy through the body with the expansion and contraction of each breath. If you are interested you can learn a lot more about breathing in *Release The Power Of Your Breath* by Long White Cloud Qigong; but for now at the beginning of your practice session taking several deep relaxed breaths paying attention to the expansion and contraction of your body with each breathe will help to prepare you to enter the flow.

Repetition

Many of the movements you will be practicing will be very simple. The purpose is to tune in to the exquisite detail of the sensation of energy in your body with each movement. This is most easily achieved with simple movements to begin with, and later this skill will flow into more complex activities. It pays to repeat movements many times, finding a natural rhythm, and little by little uncovering deeper and deeper awareness of the energy changes and flow in your body that accompany the movement. This will also allow you to refine the movement little by little as you work with this sensation of energy flow. As you progress you will be able to tap into this deeper level of awareness and refined movement more quickly and with fewer repetitions, but to begin with learn to enjoy the pleasure of refining something very simple.

Also, do not be put off if some of the movements are actually quite challenging to begin with. Again, work little by little to refine and improve the movement over many repetitions and it will become easier.

Slow Then Fast
To begin with each of the movements should be done slowly. This allows you to have greater awareness of the detail of the sensations of energy in the movement and to refine the movement through very small changes. Over time though, you can and should experiment with practicing the movements at a faster pace. It is one of the great misconceptions about qigong that it should always be done slowly. It usually begins slowly to develop awareness and skill, but over time should apply equally to fast movements. In this way you can develop different aspects of your energy and you can also bring your energy awareness and efficiency of movement into fast paced and challenging activities such as martial arts, or just use this efficiency to accomplish mundane tasks more efficiently and gracefully.

But to begin with, go slow, as slow as is comfortable for you, so that you can deepen your awareness.

Chapter Two: Playing With Waves

The first type of movement you will work with to develop and refine your awareness of energy flow in your body is wave movements. Energy naturally transfers through matter in waves. When we learn to tune into this wavelike transmission of energy through our body, we can make our movements more efficient, allowing us to accomplish more with less effort. Also as we tune into the sensations of the waves, we can feel the places where the wave transfers through smoothly and evenly and if there are any places where the energy movement is jerky or even seems to jump over some parts of our body.

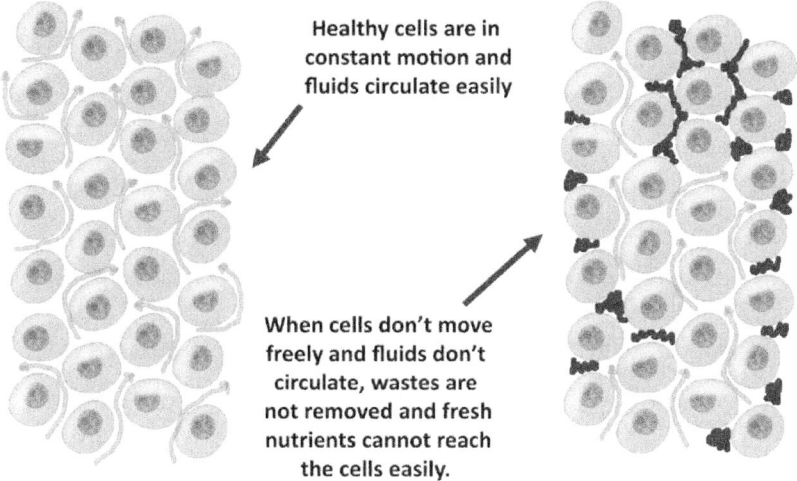

Healthy cells are in constant motion and fluids circulate easily

When cells don't move freely and fluids don't circulate, wastes are not removed and fresh nutrients cannot reach the cells easily.

The ideal is for the energy of the wave to transfer smoothly through every part of the body. This smooth wavelike transmission of energy gently massages and stimulates every cell as it moves through, helping to keep all the fluids moving in and around the cell for optimal health. If on the other hand the transmission is jerky, this indicates that there are parts of the body that are being held too stiff for the force to move through them freely. That means that the energy has to jump over these areas and they do not benefit from the gentle stimulation of energy transferring through them. Energy can quite literally become 'stuck' in these areas and fluids will not flow as freely in and around the cells, wastes will not be removed as quickly, and fresh nutrients will not be able to reach the cells as easily either.

These areas of our body which are stiff can be large or small. The energy of the wave can jump almost the whole length of our body, or the jumps or jerkiness can be much, much smaller on the cellular scale. In either of these situations as we work to make the wave of energy movement through our body smoother, we can gently soften the edges of these stiff areas and gradually get them moving freely again.

Standing Posture

Stand with your feet shoulder width apart or wider, body upright, shoulders relaxed and open, head upright as well, with the chin tucked slightly under. Sink your weight down so that your legs soften, the knees bend and your pelvis naturally tucks under a little as if you were going to sit on a stool. It should feel like your whole spine lengthens just a little when you do this, like your tailbone hangs down to the earth underneath and your head is lifted up gently from the centre towards heaven. This will be your starting posture for most of the exercises in this book.

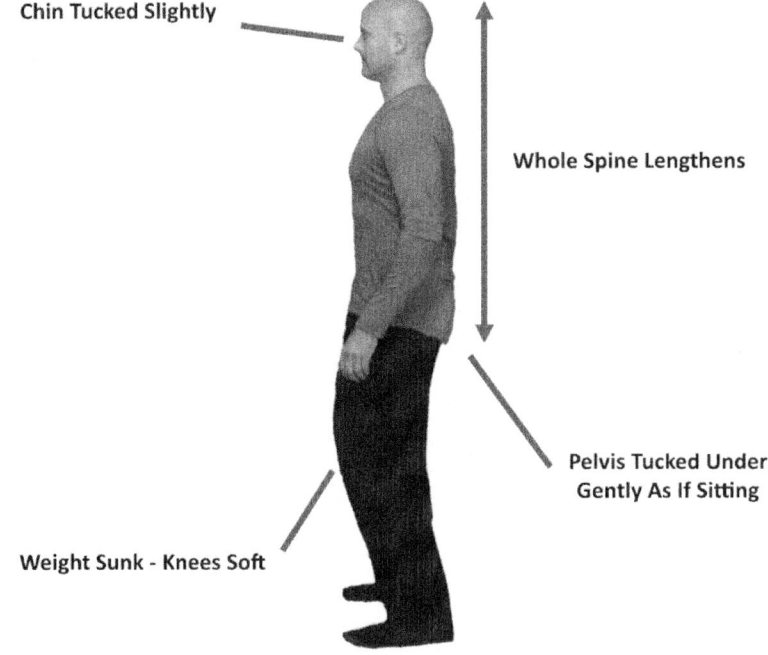

It is important to relax into this posture rather than tensing yourself into it, otherwise you defeat its purpose. It is a good idea to practice standing up straight and then relaxing into the posture several times until it feels natural for you to have your weight sunk and spine gently lengthened like this.

Rise and Fall

Breathe in and raise your arms to shoulder height.

Breathe out and lower your arms back to your sides.

Try to keep your elbows facing down as you raise and lower your arms.

As you breathe in feel your whole body fill and rise slightly straightening your legs a little.

As you breathe out feel your whole body empty and sink, softening your legs and bending your knees a little. You may feel that you want to sink deeper and deeper as you repeat this exercise.

As you breathe in, feel the wave of energy rise from the soles of your feet all the way up to shoulder height and then wash back away down through your body.

Little by little encourage the sensation of this wave of energy to become smoother and smoother as it flows through your body.

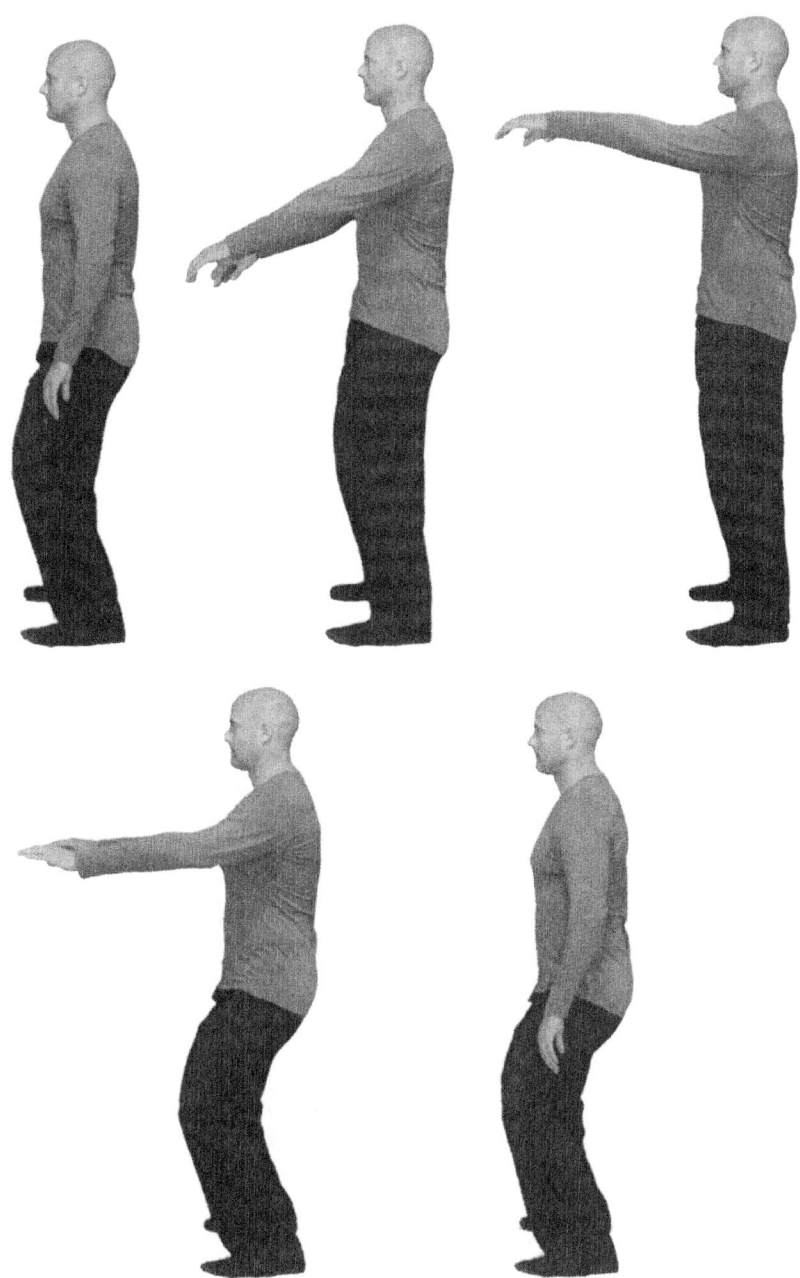

In case you are wondering. This wave of energy moving through your body is a real thing, not just something you imagine with your mind. As your arms extend away from your body and rise, the change in distribution of your weight needs to be counterbalanced through the rest of your body. This sends tension through your muscles and connective tissue and compressive forces onto your bones. These forces change as you continue to move your arms, and this change in tension stimulates the movement of fluid through your body.

These forces are subtle. They are not as obvious as the tension in the muscles of your arm as you pick up a heavy weight, but they are still there. With practice you can tune in your awareness to feel these changing forces in your body quite clearly. When you can feel the forces you are able to fine tune the functioning of your body to make it smoother and more efficient.

As these changing pressures move through your body they stimulate the nerves as they move past them, increasing the electrical activity. They also stimulate the activity of the cells by massaging them and increasing the movement of fluid around them. This leads to greater cellular activity and more heat being generated. So with practice it is not just physical force that you move through your body, but every type of energy moves together in the wave.

Rolling Waves – Forward and Back

In this movement there is both a rise and fall and forward and back shift occurring. The overall effect is a rolling motion like a wave crashing on the shore then sucking back out and rising up before rolling in to crash on the beach once more. This imagery of a rolling wave can help you to make the movement of energy in your own body smoother and more natural.

Rolling Waves - Instructions

Breathe in raising your arms to shoulder height and drawing your hands back towards your shoulders, palms facing out. You will naturally rise a little as you do this.

Breathe out pushing your hands forwards, sinking your weight and softening your knees.

Repeat

Lift Up Pour Down

Breathe in, turn your palms up, fingers pointing towards each other, and raise them close to the front of your body. As they reach the height of your shoulders you will naturally need to rotate the hands outwards so the fingers face away from each other. As the hands travel above the head, continue to rotate them outward until the fingers face each other again. Allow your weight to naturally rise, straightening your legs a little as you do this.

Breathe out, turn your palms down and lower them back in front of your body until they rest at your sides. Allow yourself to naturally sink and soften your knees with this movement and out breath.

Repeat

In this exercise the rise and fall extends further than in the earlier exercise, rising all the way up through the neck and head and arms and out through the palms of the hands before lowering down again. The overall effect can feel deeply cleansing, like lifting up water from the earth and then letting it wash back down through your whole body from the sky.

Chapter Three: Empty and Full

In this chapter your focus will shift to moving energy smoothly in your legs. Our legs act as one of our main pumps of energy and fluid through our bodies. If our lifestyle is healthy our legs are constantly active, standing and walking and circulating energy. Because of their role in supporting the rest of our body, they need to be able to cope with a lot of weight and therefore a lot of energy moving through them. Sometimes because of their constant use we get into bad habits of keeping the legs full of energy all the time. This results in heavy, stiff and inflexible legs, the effects of which quickly spread to the back and the rest of the body.

Like every other part of the body, the legs need alternating stimulation from yin to yang, full to empty, in order to stay healthy and strong. In practical terms full means to load weight on the legs with the accompanying muscle and nerve activity. Empty means to take the weight out of the leg and relax the muscles and nerves. It is common to become stuck somewhere in between, never completely filling the leg and activating the muscles and nerves effectively, and also when emptying it to never fully release the nerve and muscle activity even when the weight is off the leg, effectively making it work more than it needs to as if it was under load.

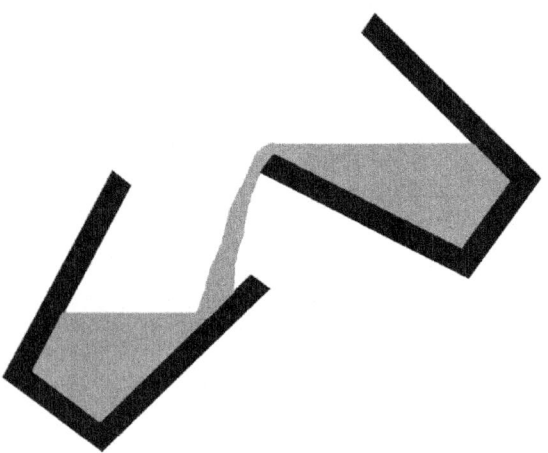

The exercises in this chapter will work on shifting the weight smoothly from one leg to the other filling one up while the other empties. You can think of this a bit like pouring water from one cup to another and back again. We want to do this smoothly so that we don't lose any of the water by sloshing it around too much. This smoothness of energy and weight transfer encourages the connective tissue to be supple and responsive and greatly improves the balance and flexibility of the legs and also the lower back. This then has a flow on effect to the rest of the body.

Side to Side

Stand with your feet wider than shoulder width apart. Keep your body and head upright and shoulders relaxed and open. You may want to put your hands on your hips as you do this exercise.

Sink your weight. You will find it much easier to transfer your weight smoothly if it is sunk than if you have it held high. If you keep your weight held high it will feel like it rocks or falls from side to side rather than gliding or rolling smoothly.

Slowly and gently shift your weight across to one leg 'filling' it up while 'emptying' the other. Make this movement as smooth as you can. Little by little move your legs further apart as it becomes comfortable for you to shift your weight smoothly from side to side.

Repeat.

Side to Side part two – lifting the legs

If you have completely emptied one leg and filled the other, the empty leg should feel light and easy to lift. Lift the knee of the empty leg as high as you can before setting it down and out to the side again, so that you can shift your weight to it and empty the leg that was previously full.

Repeat

Turning

With your legs wide apart, shift your weight across to one leg. Turn the foot of the empty leg inward towards your centreline.

Shift your weight back across onto this leg with the inward facing foot, turning your hips and shoulders as you shift your weight.

Your weight should now sit fully on the leg with the inward turned foot, with your hips and shoulders facing towards your empty leg. Turn the foot of the empty leg outward to face in the same direction as your hips and shoulders, resting on the heel with the toes pointing up.

Turn the foot of the empty leg back in so that you can repeat the process and shift your weight and turn to face the opposite direction.

Keep your body and head upright and shoulders open throughout this process.

Repeat, turning side to side transferring the weight smoothly.

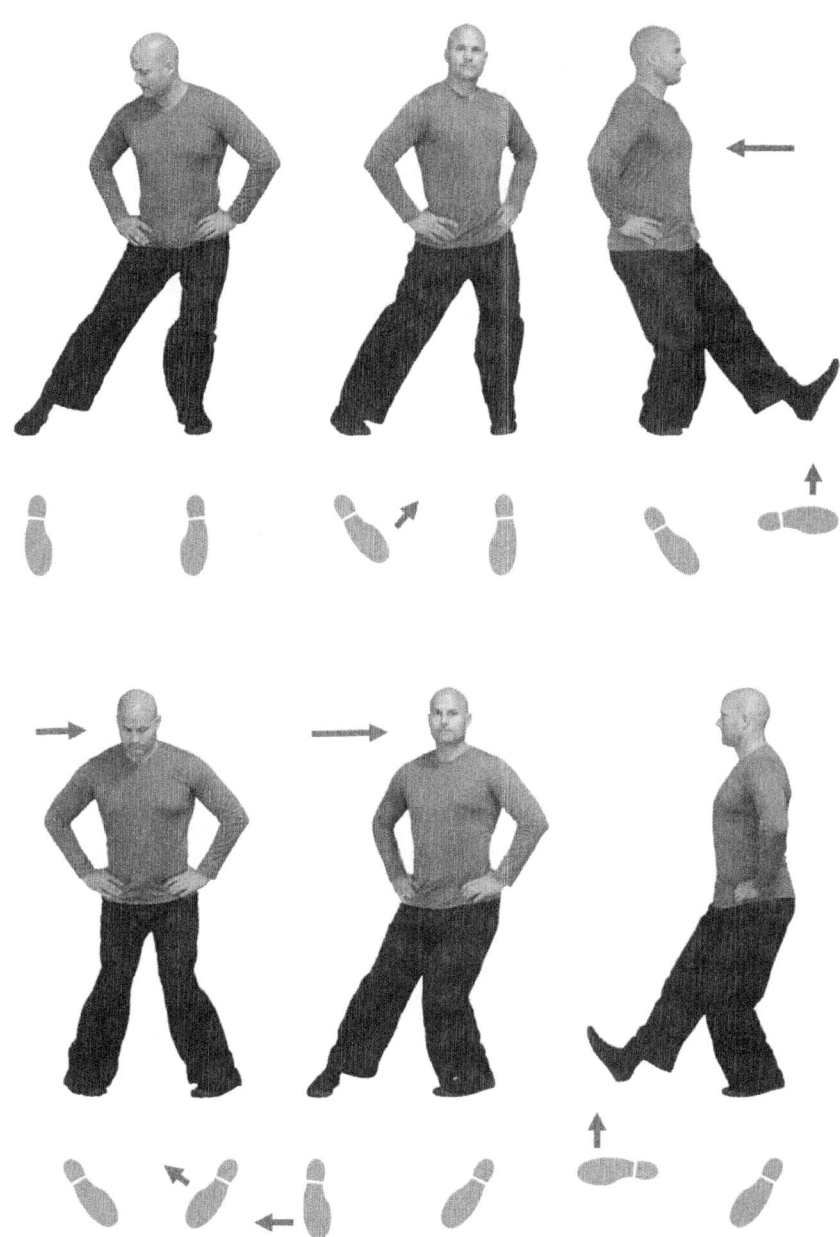

Forward and Back

After turning to one side, breathe out and transfer your weight and energy into the leg in front of you, filling it up.

Breathe in and smoothly shift the weight to the back leg.

Keep your body and head upright and your shoulders open.

Repeat.

Part two – lifting the legs

If you have completely emptied one leg and filled the other, the empty leg should feel light and easy to lift. Lift the knee of the empty leg as high as you can before setting it back down.

Transfer your weight and energy to the other leg to fill it up and try lifting the newly emptied leg.

Repeat, shifting your weight forwards and back.

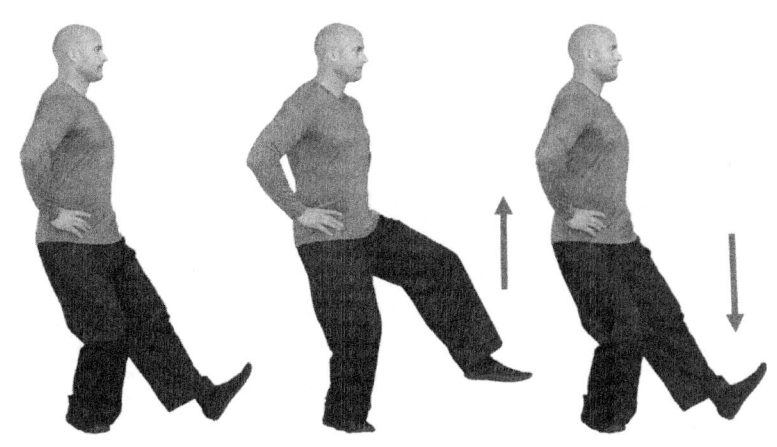

Walking

Now that you have practiced shifting your weight side to side, front and back, lifting your legs, and turning; you can put all of these together into a walking practice.

The aim is to transfer the weight from leg to leg very smoothly with awareness of emptying each leg before you lift it, and completely filling the other leg that your weight rests on. At any point in the walking you should be able to pause without wobbling and feeling out of balance. This can be a big challenge to begin with!

As mentioned earlier, many of us have habits of not completely filling and emptying our legs. This leaves us perpetually off-balance as we move about during our regular activities. Instead of transferring our weight and energy smoothly and gracefully from one leg to the other, we essentially 'fall' from step to step. This puts more strain and impact on our connective tissue and joints than is necessary, and overtime wears your body out little by little.

Learning to smoothly empty and fill your legs completely will help you to move more gracefully and efficiently and will help you to avoid injury and keep your body healthy and strong for longer!

Transfer your weight to one leg, slowly and smoothly lift the other and set it down where you want to put it – forwards, to the side, turned in whatever direction you wish to walk. Transfer your weight again and repeat.

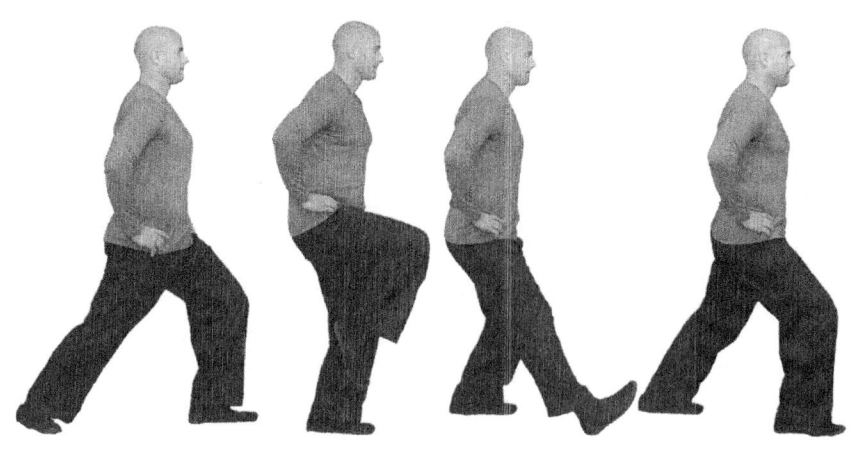

Qigong walking can be very enjoyable. By using specific movements we can stimulate the energy flows in different ways for different benefits. Little by little we can also make our qigong walking appear more like 'normal' walking, even though internally we are doing a lot more to circulate and stimulate our energy than we would with 'normal' walking. The rhythmic nature of walking means that we are easily able to practice circulating our energy in this way for long periods of time as we go about our regular activities. If you would like to learn more about this type of practice, check out *Qigong Walking* by Long White Cloud Qigong.

Combinations

Having practiced moving the energy more smoothly in your legs, you can now practice these movements in combination with the wave movements from the previous chapter. This will be the pattern as you continue on in subsequent chapters, to take the new skills and movements that you have developed and combine them with previous movements, gradually increasing the repertoire and combinations of movements that you are able to feel the smooth flow of energy through your body with.

You can combine the movements in any way that feels good to you to experiment with keeping the energy flowing smoothly through your body. A couple of simple examples.

1. Try practicing rise and fall while also lifting the legs.
2. Try practicing rolling wave as you shift your energy forwards and backwards as well.

In this way you get more of your body working together in more sophisticated ways moving the energy.

Rise and Fall

Rolling Waves

Chapter Four: Swimming Dragon

We will now look at several more movements we can add to our repertoire that will further increase our energy awareness and when combined with our other movements will allow us to begin to play at being a swimming dragon. Chinese dragons are depicted as having long sinuous bodies that twist and turn a little bit like a snake as they swim through the mist. Their movements are graceful yet powerful. The imagery of the mist brings our attention to not only the energy inside us, but also the energy which surrounds us. As we use the imagery of the swimming dragon we tune into the energy all around us which can refresh and renew us.

Stir the Mist

Stand comfortably and raise your hands to waist height. Let your hands rest at this height with the palms facing down. Slowly start to drift your hands from side to side. To begin with you can imagine that your hands are resting on the surface of water, and as they move side to side they create ripples moving outwards.

Gradually make the movements larger until your whole body is turning side to side along with your arms. Change the imagery to being surrounded by mist. As you twist and turn side to side you stir the mist causing it to swirl around you. Feel the swirls of the mist all over your body from this turning action. Also feel the coiling and twisting of the energy inside your body.

Let the energy which surrounds you settle on your skin as you move through it, like mist or gentle dew watering the earth, let this energy refresh and renew you.

Swimming in the Mist

Stand comfortably and raise one arm behind you as you raise your other arm to the front, palms facing down.

Turn your palms up and bring your rear hand forward over your head and forwards along your extended front arm, at the same time as you draw your front hand back. Sink your whole body.

Repeat.

The movement is a mix of swimming and diving and you can use the imagery of swimming and parting your way through the mist to guide your movement.

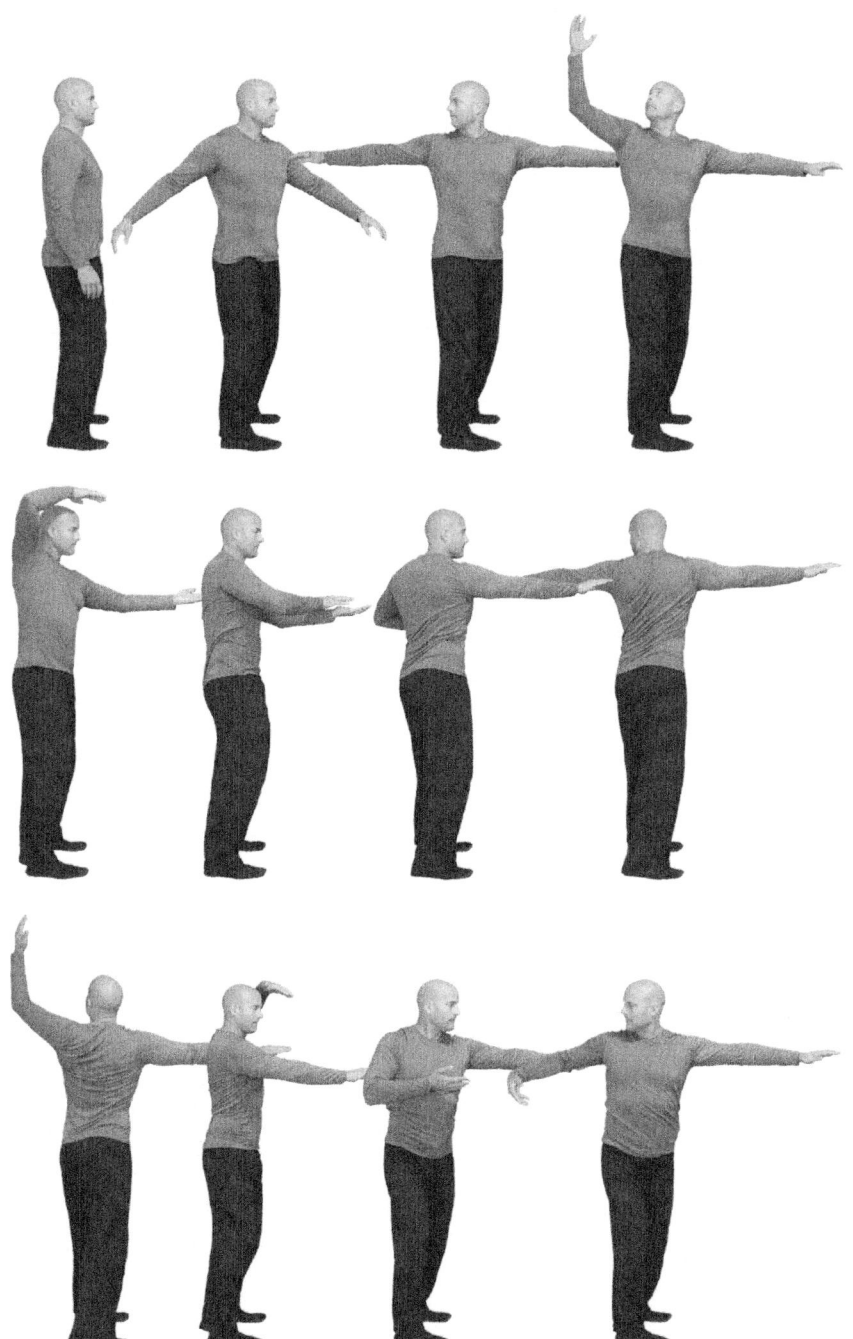

Twist and Turn

Sink your weight, place the ball of one foot across behind the other leg so that your legs are crossed.

Unwind your legs as you turn and put both feet flat on the ground again.

Repeat.

Place the heel of one foot across in front of the other leg so that your legs are crossed.

Unwind your legs as you turn and put both feet flat on the ground again.

Cross-step In Front

Cross-step Behind

Swimming Dragon

Combine these movements with the movements from earlier chapters to move like a swimming dragon through the mist. Focus on moving the energy smoothly within your body as you twist and turn and swim through the swirling mist all around you like a Chinese dragon. Feel the energy around you on your skin refreshing the energy in your body.

Chapter Five: Playing With A Ball

This chapter will explore some of the many ways that you can play with a ball of energy in your qigong. There are many movements in different qigong forms that require forming a ball of energy within the movement. Sometimes people think that this is all about having relaxed posture and using the efficiency of curved shapes within your movement, and while it is true that working with a ball shape creates these habits in your body, the point is also to actually form a ball of energy.

This may seem like an unusual thing to do if you have not practiced much qigong already, but it is really not so strange if you think about how your body works.

A lot of information is carried around your body through nerve impulses, literally electrical currents that run through your body. Wherever there is an electrical current a magnetic field is created. This is not fringe science, it is very much mainstream, everyday, normal science. It is also known that magnetic fields can contain and direct heat, sound, and systems of charged particles. So the idea that we can form a ball of energy between our hands through directing the activity of our bodies energy should not really be all that farfetched.

Measuring these fields presents more of a challenge though because in absolute terms the energy in the field is quite low, and so requires specialised equipment to register it and measure it accurately. In absolute terms the strength of the energy fields we create is relatively weak, but their power and usefulness comes from the way that they combine many different types of living energy together in a uniquely human way. So while some scientific work has been done on measuring these fields, this has focused on just measuring one aspect at a time – which is useful of course, but does not capture a very complete picture of these fields.

Scientific equipment may not yet be up to the task of fully recording and measuring our natural energy fields, but each of us has our own unique apparatus which is fully capable of detecting all of the subtleties of them. This of course is your own body, the same thing that generates the field. It may take quite a bit of time and practice to develop this skill and awareness, but little by little you can come to perceive and understand these fields for yourself while we wait for external technology to catch up with our own innate abilities.

Practicing generating a ball of energy has significant tangible benefits. In order to form a strong ball of energy you need to generate and sustain a strong flow of energy within your body too. This means that there needs to be good nerve conductivity, good blood flow, and good cellular activity. The strength of the energy field we can create acts as a feedback mechanism that lets us know how well we are able to flow energy through our body, and as we practice making the field stronger we increase our ability to flow energy more strongly too. This means we further strengthen our nerves and improve our ability to circulate blood and so on.

To begin with you will work on forming and working with a ball, because it is the shape that is easiest for us to form naturally. But later on you may wish to experiment with forming the field into other shapes as well.

When you have developed awareness and skill with this energy that you generate, you can use it for many different purposes, one of the most common of which is healing, both of yourself and others. If you are interested in learning more about this aspect of qigong, you might like to check out *Introduction to Qigong Healing* from Long White Cloud Qigong.

Forming a Ball

There are several methods you can use for this depending on how relaxed you are, how strong your energy flow is, and how developed your energy awareness is. You can try each of these to see what works for you. As you continue to practice it will get easier and easier to form a bay of energy between your hands.

Method One: Gathering the Mist

Practice stirring the mist for a few moments as described in the previous chapter. Then change the pattern of movements with your arms slightly, so that instead of just stirring and swirling side to side, you gather the energy around you together in front of you to form a ball. You can think of this a little like gathering snow to form a snowball.

You then roll your hands around the outside of the ball, further defining its edges and strengthening it through sending more energy out into it.

If you have already developed good awareness of energy, and are relaxed and have your energy flowing strongly, you will be able to do this quickly and easily. If on the other hand you are a bit tense, or your awareness is not developed yet, this method may be quite difficult for you and you may need to use method two instead.

This method of gathering the mist is gentler and requires less of your own energy to form the ball as you also draw on the energy around you to do this, you can also do it very quickly when you have developed sufficient skill with it, so this should be your preferred way of forming a ball if possible.

Gather the energy together in front of you

Then roll your hands around the outside of it forming a ball

Method Two: Clapping and Rubbing

The second method is to clap your hands vigorously together to activate the nerves in your hands and make them tingle, and then rub your hands vigorously to make them warm and make the cells more active. This increased activity naturally means more energy flow in your hands and therefore the start of an energy field.

Next hold your palms close together and see if you can feel the energy radiating out from one hand to the other. Move the hands a little further apart and then a little closer together feeling the magnetism and heat between your hands. Gradually move your hands further apart and when they are far enough apart to form a ball shape between them start to roll your hands around the ball as in method one.

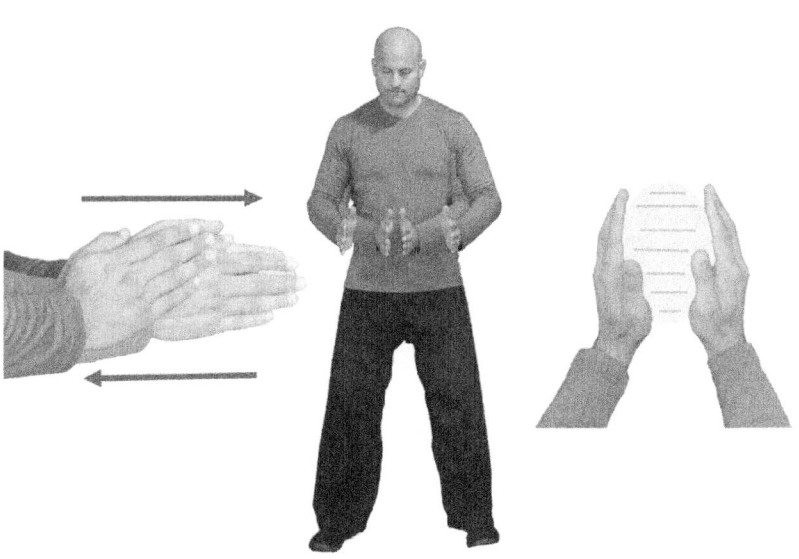

Rub yours hands together and clap them vigorously, then feel the energy between your hands.

Then form a ball between your hands.

While many people will be able to feel their radiated energy and form a ball quite quickly using this method, don't be too concerned if you cannot feel a ball straight away. For some people it will take some practice to get their body relaxed enough and their mind clear enough to let their energy flow and be aware of the field it creates. If you can't feel the energy field straight away, just continue to practice the other qigong exercises in this book, and return to forming a ball from time to time to see how you are progressing until you can do this easily.

One of the common mistakes people make when starting to do this sort of exercise, is that when they are successful in starting to feel their energy, they then concentrate too hard on it trying to strengthen the field. When we concentrate very hard we have a tendency to hold our breath and to tense our muscles. Doing this then starts to decrease the flow of energy due to reduced oxygen levels in the blood and pressure on the nerves and blood vessels from the muscle tension. So while of course you need to concentrate, it needs to be a relaxed kind of concentration where you remember to keep breathing and to allow the tissues of your body to be relaxed but active so that the energy can flow.

If you find that you are able to form a ball, but then lose awareness of it after awhile, relax, let go of the awareness of the ball. Maybe shake your arms out or do some of the basic rise and fall exercise to release any excess tension, and then begin again to form a new ball. Over time this will become easier and easier for you to maintain.

Also, it probably pays to note that the environment you practice in will make a big difference to your ability to form a ball to begin with. The amount of distractions around you will affect how easily you are able to stay relaxed and focused to direct your energy. But other physical factors will also make a big difference. For example, if it is quite windy it will be much harder for your field to keep heat and charged particles contained. They will literally blow away and make it much harder for you to maintain your field. Also if it is very cold, you will find it much harder to generate sufficient heat to make your field feel warm, as your body will be working hard just to keep itself warm let alone sending heat out into the field as well.

Finally, it is very important when working with generating fields outside of your body that you take some time when you finish practicing to return the focus of your energy flow from outside to inside your body. As mentioned already, the field we create is made up of real energy, not just the thoughts of your mind, so it takes real effort to build and maintain it. If you do not take the time to return your focus inward, you can easily be left running energy out of your body which will drain you over time.

It is very simple to return this focus by simply taking the energy ball and drawing it into your lower dantien. Your dantien is the centre of your body where you naturally store energy. It is located a few inches below your belly button and in the centre of your body. When you return the energy you sent out into your field to your centre you store it up for future use. Leave your hands resting above your dantien for a few moments to settle your energy before returning to your normal activities.

Holding a Ball

Having formed a ball, your next challenge is to simply hold that ball. To begin with it is easier to maintain a ball by keeping your hands constantly moving around it, as the movement stimulates the flow of energy from your centre and down through your arms, and helps to keep them from getting too tense. It is a little more difficult to simply hold the ball, but in doing so you will learn to keep the flow of energy open without having to rely on physical movement.

If you find that your ball starts to weaken, you can start moving your hands again for awhile and focus on strengthening it by sending energy out from your centre through your arms with your breath, and then return to simply holding the ball again when you are ready.

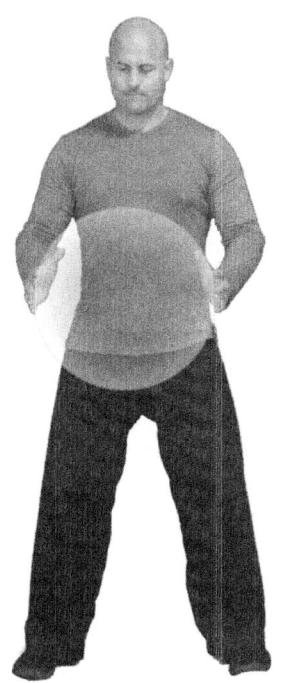

Lifting and Lowering

In this next exercise, you will maintain the shape and size of the ball while lifting and lowering it, to become even more skilled at maintaining the flow of energy and awareness while moving your body in different ways.

Start by lifting the ball straight up and then down again. Only move as quickly as you are able to maintain your awareness of the ball. To begin with this will probably need to be very slow, but over time you will be able to do this more quickly.

After lifting the ball up and down, you can also try lifting it up to each side. As you do this you will find that it challenges and stretches your back and other parts of your body in different ways while you focus on maintaining the flow of energy.

Holding to Each Side

In this exercise you will hold the ball a little differently. Roll your hands around the ball until one hand rests comfortably on top of it, and the other supports it from below. Bring the ball around to the same side of your body as the hand that supports it from below. You may notice that your arms naturally curve around the ball a little more in this position so that your wrists also press against the ball and support it.

Bring the ball back in front of you and roll your hands around so that they switch positions and then move the ball to hold on the other side of your body.

Repeat, moving the ball from side to side and alternating which hand is on top and which hand is on the bottom of the ball.

Holding a Large Ball

Roll your hands around the ball gradually making it bigger and bigger until it is very large, then wrap your arms around the ball and pull it in closer to you. Sink your weight and bend your knees to create a solid support for holding the ball.

In this position you will have contact with the ball all along the inside of your arms and against your chest. This should feel quite nice. Also, all of the structures of your body, your arms, shoulders, torso and legs will align as if they are holding something heavy. Flowing energy through the tissues while they are aligned in this way will create good habits make them stronger and more capable of supporting something that is actually heavy without straining.

Holding a Ball in One Hand

Form a ball and roll your hands around it as you usually would. Bring your hands to a position holding the ball with one hand on top and the other below. Take the top hand away and see if you can maintain your awareness of the ball resting on top of just one hand as you move this hand around.

Repeat using the other hand.

Bouncing and Throwing

Form a ball and then practice bouncing it on the ground and then feel it return to your hands. You can also try throwing it up in the air and then letting it drop back into your hands.

This is another exercise that might stretch your understanding of what your body and mind is capable of in directing energy outside of your body. But play with it and practice it and you will be able to feel it for yourself and understand it innately without having to comprehend every intellectual detail of how you are able to do this.

Combinations

As in previous chapters, once you have become comfortable with these different exercises playing with a ball, you can combine them with movements from the previous chapters. For example you might try walking while carrying a large ball. Or you might quickly form a ball while moving through the mist as a swimming dragon, and play with moving it from one hand to the other as you twist and turn. The possibilities are limitless.

Chapter Six: Fighting Movements

One of the areas that qigong and energy awareness has historically been most famously applied to is martial arts. The epitome of this is Taiji (also spelled Tai Chi) with the predominance of gentle flowing movements in its training methodology, but Bagua, Xing Yi and in fact every style of Kung Fu utilizes principles of qigong if you delve far enough into them.

The benefits are clear, having a greater understanding of how your mind and body work together gives you tools for optimizing your performance to operate at peak levels, which of course is very important when facing potentially life and death situations. Further understanding the functioning of your opponent's mind and body opens up the possibility of many different strategies and tactics that can be used to defeat them.

Accomplished martial artists with extraordinary reflexes, speed, endurance and physical resilience can be great examples of the potential of qigong to enhance your performance and general health and wellbeing, but at the same time I think it is a bit of a shame that the association between qigong and martial arts is so strong. Because of this strong historic connection some people go so far as to assume that qigong is itself a martial art, which it clearly is not. Qigong is much, much broader than that, and can be applied to every area of your life.

You don't need to be interested in the art of fighting in order to take up and benefit from qigong practice. But... there are also good reasons why you might want to spend at least a little time exploring how qigong applies to fighting movements.

Fighting is stressful. When we use fighting movements, on a deep level there is an implication to our unconscious mind that there is some threat to our wellbeing that could seriously harm us. The natural tendency when we feel under threat or stressed is to tense up our body to brace it and protect it from injury. As mentioned in an earlier chapter, when we tense too much this tends to cut off the flow of energy through our bodies, leading to long term degeneration. By practicing maintaining energy flow in the stressful situation of fighting we develop a skill that can then extend into other areas of our lives, helping us to maintain that flow in whatever situation we face.

So in this chapter we are going to explore a few fighting movements and see if we can keep our energy flowing throughout them. You may notice that you begin to tense subtley to brace your body as you even begin to think about a movement as being used for fighting. Relax and find the flow within the movement. Tune into the sensation of energy within the movement and make this as fluid and smooth as you can. Start by doing each movement slowly, and then gradually speed up still focusing on the fluid movement of energy moving in waves through your body. If you are successful at this, over time you will be able to do the movements with more speed and power than if you did not take the time to tune into and be aware of the energy flow.

Some of the movements we will use are intentionally very linear. Sometimes people have a misconception that in order for energy to flow movements need to be obviously circular. This is not true. Even what appear to be very linear movements will have elements of circularity within them, and the energy can flow just as easily if you find them. They are more challenging to feel the flow though, which makes them perfect for our practice of this principle.

Punching

Stand in a bow stance. This means you have one foot forward, the front knee bent, and the back leg quite straight with the foot turned out to the side on an angle somewhere between 0 and 90 degrees.

Draw your hands back by your waist, hands in fists and the palm side facing up.

Breathe out as you extend one fist forward turning the fist over so the palm side faces down.

Don't concentrate on the in breath, just let it come in quickly at the end of the punch.

Breathe out again as you extend the other hand forward and pull your front hand back to its start position.

Repeat several times, concentrating on the fluidity of the movement and the sense of energy flowing up and out from the centre of your body and the earth beneath you with each punch.

Repeat with your other leg forward.

Kicking

Stand in a bow stance, hands guarding in front of you. Shift your weight forward onto your front leg. Lift your knee high in front of you. Breathe out as you extend your foot forward in a kicking action.

Return your leg to its starting position.

Repeat using your other leg.

See if you can have a sense of fluidity and flow of energy throughout the movement.

Blocking

Stand with feet shoulder width apart or wider, hands guarding in front of you. Turn the palm of one hand up and open the arm out to shoulder width with the elbow facing down. Bring the other hand back to rest by the elbow with the palm facing down.

Repeat with the other hand.

Throwing

Stand in a bow stance, hands guarding in front of you. Reach forwards closing your hands as if grabbing something. Turn your hips, pivot your feet and shift your weight so that your bow stance now faces the other way, pressing your hands forwards.

Feel the flow of energy through your whole body as you do this.

Repeat in the other direction.

Shadow Fighting

Imagine you are fighting an imaginary opponent. You can use the movements you have already practiced, and any other fighting movements you are familiar with or that come to mind.

Imagine your opponent attacking you with kicks, punches and trying to grab you. Respond by blocking, kicking, punching, dodging and throwing your imaginary opponent. Do this in slow motion to begin with, concentrating on the sense of energy flow in your body. Gradually speed up and see if you can maintain this sense of energy flow.

This chapter has looked at only a few fighting movements for you to practice feeling the flow of energy in. The purpose is to help you to understand the value of applying energy awareness to a stressful type of activity. If you would like to learn more fighting movements and how to apply them effectively I would suggest learning a martial art in depth – which is well beyond the scope of this book. There are many options to choose from, and I am sure you will be able to find something in your area to learn. If you do decide to learn a martial art, see if you can bring your awareness of energy into your movements every time you practice.

Chapter Seven: Everyday Movements

In the last chapter we looked at applying energy awareness to the very stressful situation of fighting. But this is not the only stressful situation we face in life. Hopefully for most of us we will face real violence very rarely or not at all. But all of us face much more mundane stresses on a regular basis as we go about our normal activities.

Sometimes the stress is to do with the activity at hand, often it is more generalised stress which may have nothing to do with our current activity. If we are stressed about the activity we may over tense our muscles reducing or cutting off the energy flow. If the stress is more generalized it may be more that we just lose awareness of our body, and use it in unbalanced and inefficient ways which are more likely to tire and damage our bodies.

We can use the principles of being aware of energy flow that we have applied to other types of movements and apply them to our everyday activities. As we reconnect with the sensations of our body and focus on energy flow we will naturally adjust our posture, alignment of joints, muscle tension, nerve activity and blood circulation to allow our energy to reach every part of our body. When we do this, even the most mundane activity can become very enjoyable as there is great pleasure in simply experiencing your own body functioning efficiently and healthily.

You may find it is quite difficult to feel the flow of energy in many of your regular activities due to poor habits of mind and body with regard to those activities. You may find that you need to go very slowly to begin with in order to feel the energy flow, and in the process discover many aches and pains and things that don't feel quite right in your body. This can be quite uncomfortable, and the natural tendency when we become aware of too many uncomfortable things is to just let go of our awareness of them again so we don't have to truly experience the discomfort. But it is worth it! Little by little you can make adjustments to relieve each area of discomfort in your body and improve the energy flow through it. Start by focusing on one area of your body at a time as you work with different activities. Once you can feel the energy flowing easily through that area, you can move on to another area, until you can feel energy flow throughout your whole body.

As you are successful in creating healthy energy flow through more and more of your body, each activity becomes more and more efficient. You will also be able to do the activity faster and more efficiently while focusing on the flow of energy, as your body starts to work in a more effective way. So, what starts out as a slow process focusing on yours inner awareness in the end can help you to accomplish the external tasks you need to do more quickly and without causing stiffness, fatigue, or possible injury.

We will look briefly at a few different activities for you to try as examples, but you can try applying energy awareness and flow to any of your normal activities. It is particularly beneficial to develop this awareness and skill with activities that you do a lot of and need to get done efficiently, activities that you find yourself getting stiff and sore from, or activities that you don't enjoy.

With practice you can turn any activity into an enjoyable moving meditation that is good for both your mind and body, while accomplishing things you need to get done at the same time!

Sweeping

This is a great activity to apply energy awareness and conscious movement to. Your whole body is involved in this movement. There is the pushing of the broom which will have similarities to the *Rolling Waves* movement in chapter two, but it is not just your arms that will be moving. Your legs and body will need to be behind the movement as well, so there will be similarities to the *Empty and Full* and *Walking* from chapter three. You will find that holding and pushing the broom also requires rotation of your torso, so there will be elements of the *Stir the Mist* exercise in chapter five.

You will need to combine all of these together into one harmonious flow of movement and awareness through your body. Becoming aware of all the parts working together, while achieving the task at hand of tiding up an area of floor or ground.

With practice this whole body action and awareness can become deeply meditative. Of course, you could also try vacuuming as an activity with a similar movement dynamic.

Washing Dishes

This activity involves mainly the arms, but to get the best sense of energy flow, you will need to still use and have awareness of your whole body. If you try to just concentrate on flow in one part of your body, the flow will be quite weak as the natural way for energy to flow is through the whole body. If you focus on the flow in just one area, that flow has to connect with the rest of the body and when it reaches an area that is not flowing its continued movement will be restricted.

So even though you may be standing relatively still while washing the dishes, see if you can get a sense of the energy in your whole body circulating and flowing with each movement. Similar to the *Stir the Mist* exercise in chapter five, even if your feet stay in the same position, there will be changes in the forces and energy running through them as you turn side to side, forward and back and move your arms. The movements of your hands when washing the dishes will be much smaller than those you made while Stirring the Mist, but you can still tune into the effect of them in activating the energy and making it swirl and move throughout your whole body.

Typing

This activity is even more challenging to feel the energy flow within because the movements of your hands are even smaller, and now you are likely to be seated, so the movement and change of forces through the rest of your body are likely to be even more subtle.

When you first try this it may help to spend some time increasing the flow of energy to your hands and becoming aware of it before you then apply this to typing. You can use the same clapping and rubbing type of stimulation that you used in chapter four when Forming a Ball. You might like to do some basic Rise and Fall to get a sense of your energy moving through your whole body as well, before you then tune in to the energy movement and flow throughout your whole body caused by each individual finger moving as you type.

Yes a movement as small as a single finger moving can and should stir the energy throughout the whole body when you are completely healthy and the energy is flowing freely. It is this connection through the whole body that is the basis for healing arts such as acupuncture and reflexology. Activity in even the smallest part of your body can stimulate the flow in even the most distant parts from it.

One of the keys to allowing the energy to flow will be to pay attention to your posture as you sit. If you are too slouched or too stiff, the tension will restrict the flow of energy to your hands. So if you find that your energy awareness and flow in your hands starts to decrease, take few moments to move your body around gently and adjust your posture. See if you can reconnect with a sense of the energy in the rest of your body and then direct it to flow back out to your hands.

Driving

This presents another new challenge. Similar to typing you are likely to be seated and the movements with your hands and arms a likely to be quite small. The new challenge is one of awareness. When you are driving, a lot of your attention needs to be on what is going on around you on the road. Your challenge will be to maintain awareness of your own body and energy, even while you have something else important to pay attention to. In this way, your energy awareness will become a kind of 'background' awareness that you can maintain in many situations in life.

Chapter Eight: Freestyle Qigong

Having practiced feeling the flow of energy in your body with a variety of different specific movements, it is now time to expand your practice of energy awareness and flow to include EVERY kind of movement. In freestyle qigong you are free to explore any kind of movement that you wish, the only guiding principle is that you focus on maintaining an awareness of healthy energy flow throughout your body as you practice. The possibilities of different types of movement are literally infinite. You are limited only by your own creativity and inspiration.

Activating Your Energy

Many people find having such wide open possibility daunting to begin with. This is why we began this book with simple specific movements for you to practice and gain experience with feeling your energy flow within, before opening up to the limitless possibilities of freestyle qigong. As you start to practice your qigong in a more freestyle way it is helpful to follow this same pattern. To start your sessions with simple and familiar movements that will help you to activate and tune into your energy flow so that you can feel it clearly and get yourself into a state of mind and body that will make it easier for you to continue to feel that energy flow in your movements rather than to start moving in a freestyle way and hope that the energy awareness will follow.

I always find that practicing a little 'rise and fall' and perhaps some 'stir the mist' is a great way to tune into the movement of energy in my body quickly and easily before doing some freestyle qigong, but you could also practice complete sets of other qigong exercises you are familiar with to activate your energy flow before moving into some freestyle practice. The 'Twelve Rivers' or 'Between Heaven and Earth' practices from Long White Cloud Qigong are great for activating your internal energy so that you can feel it more easily. Alternatively you could do some Zhan Zhuang standing practice from 'Movement In

Stillness' to activate your energy before moving into freestyle qigong movements.

Ways to Work With The Energy Flow

Once you have the energy active so that you can feel the energy moving through your body, there are many ways you can work with it. You can use large movements such as 'playing with waves', 'swimming in the mist', or several of the other movements looked at in this book, or you can use very small movements like those used in washing the dishes or typing. Even just moving one finger can stimulate the movement of energy throughout the rest of your body when you are relaxed and centred. With practice you can come to feel and direct the movement of energy from even very small and subtle movements.

You may even want to experiment with sometimes being still as part of your freestyle qigong. This stillness should never be complete stillness though. The energy should move within it. In this way the stillness becomes like moments of silence within music. They serve an active purpose in transitions between the other notes played and become like a note themselves. Integrating stillness into your freestyle qigong can be a way to work with transitions of movement of energy in your body. When you move and then your movement comes to rest externally, you can allow the energy to continue to move internally 'completing' the movement of the energy more fully internally before perhaps changing direction into a new movement. The pause of stillness can allow the energy to transition and even build momentum into the next movement.

You might like to also play with the rhythm and speed of your movements. You can experiment with moving very slowly, at more moderate speeds, and also very quickly. This will allow you to observe and to build skill with your energy flow at different speeds of movement and to become more proficient at moving between them. You can also establish different patterns of rhythm within your movement to see how these feel to you and which you are more comfortably with. Your qigong can start to look a lot like dancing, and this is a good analogy for how your energy can feel when you become skilled with it. Everything feels like it is dancing on the inside, with enjoyment, gracefulness and pleasure, rather than with clumsiness, irritability, and discomfort.

You may find as you practice freestyle qigong that you want to continually change your movement. Constantly exploring new movements, rhythms and speeds. Alternatively you may also find that you want to repeat the same movement or sequence of movements over and over again, feeling the flow of energy through that particular movement repeatedly. Both are fine, and which you feel inclined to do will often be largely determined by what purpose you bring to your qigong practice session.

Purposeful Practice
It is very helpful to have a purpose in mind each time you practice qigong. Without a purpose your session can feel aimless and may not actually be particularly helpful to you. With no direction, your energy flow may not accomplish anything useful. By choosing a purpose as you begin your session, you will change the way you practice. Even if you just set your purpose and then essentially forget about it as you proceed into your practice, unconsciously you will change the way that you practice towards achieving that purpose. Even practicing movements that look almost identical, at a deep level you will change the way that you do the movement to alter the energy flow and the effect that it has on you.

There are many different types of purpose that you could choose to have for your practice sessions. It could be as simple as learning a new movement or making a movement smoother so that the energy can flow more freely when you do it. This is largely what you will have been doing as you have practiced the different exercises in this book so far, but now as you open yourself to the possibility of an infinite variety of movements, you can also choose other types of purpose for your practice.

Creativity and Self Expression

Your purpose can be as simple as to enjoy the sensation of energy moving in your body. If we tune into the pleasurable sensations of our bodies we can use this to make positive changes by increasing the healthy functioning that cause these. You can simply explore moving in ways that make the energy flow feel good to you.

There aren't really any rules for this, you simply start making movements and see what they do to your energy and then 'follow' the energy wherever it feels good to go next. It is a little bit like an artist doodling. Sometimes they might just draw a lot of lines and curves that don't really mean much, or simply have a pleasing pattern. Other times within their doodling they may discover the start of ideas for something they would like to draw, or different ways of doing things.

Similarly in your qigong practice you may find at times that this intention of enjoying the sensation of energy moving in your body is just fun and enjoyable. Other times it may act as a source of inspiration to you, revealing different ways that your body wants to move in that you may not have been allowing it to, or types of movement that you may want to explore further in a more structured way when they come to your attention.

In this way this type of practice can be a great source of creativity and an outlet of self expression for you. It is interesting how many people are very shy about freeing themselves to move in any way they want to, even when they are completely alone with no-one else watching. They often still have ideas about needing to do things 'properly' or doing the 'right' kind of movement that will look a certain way.

I think this is very revealing of just how much we are inclined to judge ourselves on a deep level all of the time. When you practice in this way, try to be truly open to moving in whatever way feels good to you. When we allow ourselves to move past this self judgement and be truly free to move in any way we wish, we can discover things about ourselves and our bodies that may surprise us. This sense of freedom can help us to make positive changes in our movement and our lives.

Healing Injury and Illness

Another purpose you could bring to your qigong practice could be to overcome injury or illness. You might identify an area of your body that is stiff, weak, or painful, and come to your practice session with the intention of relieving or resolving the issues there.

As you practice you would keep your awareness on that area as you do different movements and notice how the different movements feel and affect the energy flow through that area. You might notice that some movements feel better than others and that they help to improve the energy flow, in which case you might choose to practice more of those movements, or spend time exploring variations of them. On the other hand you might continue to practice a wide variety of movements keeping your awareness on the affected area, and with each movement encourage the energy to move freely and gently start to loosen and clear any blocked energy from the area.

It is important to remember that moving any part of the body can stimulate the movement of energy through the whole of the body, so you may feel inspired to practice movements that don't seem to have any direct relationship to the area of your body that you are concerned about, but they may still be useful in helping to heal the area.

You may also find that by practicing gently and with awareness you are able to quite quickly improve the movement in an area so that you are able to perform movements that were previously to painful or too difficult because of weakness or stiffness. This is great! But always remember to be gentle with yourself and not to force yourself into challenging movements, allow your awareness of your energy flow to guide you as to what will be helpful and what will be harmful to your body.

Specific Movement Refinement

You may have specific movements that you would like to refine and make more efficient. Perhaps relating to your work, a sport you play, or just something that you enjoy. As mentioned earlier, tuning into the sensation of energy flow through your body can be a great way to improve efficiency, speed, endurance and other aspects of your physical performance, as optimal energy flow requires optimal nerve function, circulation of blood and other fluids, balance of tension, alignment of joints, distribution of load, and so on.

You can off course work to improve your energy flow in these movements by simply practicing them and using the same principles of awareness we discussed in *Chapter Seven: Everyday Movements.*

But you can also bring this into the purpose of your freestyle qigong practice.

You may find that by having improving a specific movement as your purpose for freestyle qigong, you are inspired to explore different aspects of the movement that you wouldn't be as inclined to notice or work on when performing the actual movement.

For example if you wanted to improve the efficiency and power of your tennis serve, you might find yourself stuck in a bit of a rut of doing your serve in a certain way and trying to improve the energy flow through that certain way of serving if you were to just practice energy awareness while doing the actual movement. By looking at the movement a bit more abstractly by having it as the purpose of your freestyle qigong practice, you might find yourself noticing how much power the 'rise and fall' type of energy flow can give your serve when you integrate it into your serving motion. You could notice that your waist needs to move more freely to make your serving motion more fluid and that practicing 'stirring the mist' helps you to get this happening. You could also notice nuances of the movement of your feet and spend time working specifically on this. You may also notice that you find you have stiffness in part of your shoulder, or chest, or your knee, or somewhere you hadn't really noticed before. And that you are able to resolve this through a type of movement that really doesn't seem to have anything directly to do with actually doing a tennis serve. But by having improving your serve as your purpose for your freestyle qigong practice, and allowing yourself to explore anything that comes to mind as you follow your energy flow in your session, you are able to discover it and resolve it.

Of course a tennis serve is just one example of a specific movement you may want to improve. You can use this same approach to working with any kind of movement you choose.

Energy Character Development

As you progress in your qigong practice you may come across concepts such as 'five element theory' where you associate the characteristics and feeling of different elements with the functioning of our organs and emotions. You might also encounter styles of qigong where you imitate the movements of animals and take on their characteristics. These types of practice develop the character of our energy in different ways. You can find specific qigong practices that utilize these principles in *Wild Animal Play* from Long White Cloud Qigong, but you may also want to explore these principles in a more freeform way to open yourself to new understanding and creative expression of them. So you could choose to use freestyle qigong as a way to explore one or more of them.

For example, you could be interested in exploring the element of fire and its connection to tiger qigong, in which case you would set this as you purpose and allow this to gently guide your freestyle practice to help you take on the fiery energy and apply it to tiger movements. Alternatively you could want to explore the connection of water to tiger qigong, in which case with this as your purpose you would likely find yourself emphasising different movements, or possibly even practicing the same movements but with a different feeling to them to help you to discover different aspects of the tiger energy character.

More Abstract Purposes

You can also choose much more abstract things to have as your purpose for your practice sessions. For example you might choose something like to be happier, or to have a better relationship with your mother. This kind of purpose may not appear to relate directly to your practice of feeling the flow of energy within your body as you move, but as you practice, unconsciously you will uncover patterns of movements relate to the purpose.

You may find yourself discovering tensions in your body or postures that you may not have been aware of that relate to emotions or situations. You may even find yourself making movements which in a sense 'act out' actions or events that relate to your purpose. Once brought to the surface you can understand them better and use your qigong practice to allow the energy to flow freely and alter your experience of these things.

Whatever purpose we choose, when we follow the flow of energy and allow ourselves to be truly free in our movement, our unconscious can uncover blockages in our energy flow, or ways that the flow is being directed that is running counter to our purpose, and allow us to change.

Chapter Nine: Enter The Flow

The final stage in these practices is to 'Enter the Flow', to keep your energy flowing in a healthy way at all times throughout all of your activities. When we do this, healthy energy flow becomes a habit, rather than something we need to specifically 'practice'. The healthy energy flow in our bodies will help to keep us healthy and make us physically resilient and less prone to injury. The efficiency of our movements will result in higher energy levels and greater endurance in whatever we do.

Maintaining a constant state of flow may not come easily though. For most people it will be lifetime pursuit to achieve this. Gradually, little by little coming closer to constantly maintaining this state of balance and high efficiency. This chapter will provide some tips on how you can go about this.

The first tip is to make time regularly to practice qigong, including the 'Enter the Flow' practices found in this book. The more time you spend practicing being aware of your energy and encouraging it to flow freely, the more familiar this will feel to you and the more easily you will be able to enter a flow state. Make sure that you include plenty of freestyle qigong in your practice as this will allow you to explore a wide variety of movements that will make it easier to flow in the many different situations you encounter in life. Take pleasure in feeling the flow of energy in your body, then more and more being in the flow will just be associated with feeling good!

Integrate awareness of your energy flow into your daily life little by little. For example, set yourself a goal of staying in the flow for the whole time it takes to make dinner or some other activity that you do regularly. It make help to do a few exercises before you begin to tune in to your energy and get it flowing, and then see if you can maintain it. Check in every few minutes to see if you are still in the flow. You can do this by briefly scanning your body with your awareness. Can you feel the good healthy feeling of energy flow in your feet, your ankles, your legs, your pelvis, your abdomen, your chest, back, arms, hands, neck and head? If you need to, make adjustments to bring yourself back into a flow state.

Once you are comfortable staying in the flow while you complete one activity regularly, choose another activity to make your focus. Practice staying in the flow in this activity until you now have two activities that are easy for you to maintain flow within. As your repertoire of activities that you flow within grows, you can start to see if you are able to maintain a sense of flow through larger portions of time, or even your whole day. Start your day by getting into a flow state with some qigong and then see if you can maintain it. Check in every half hour or so and see if you are still flowing. If you need to, make adjustments.

You may find that there are certain activities or situations that you find really hard to maintain flow throughout. Most of these you will be able to resolve yourself by making working on these the purpose of your freestyle qigong practice sessions to help you to develop skill at flowing in these situations. But, you may find that there are some things that even with lots of practice you still have difficulty finding the flow within. In these cases it may be useful to seek help from someone else to help you identify and clear whatever it is that may be blocking your flow.

There are many things that can cause a persistent block in your flow. These can include postural and body use habits that you are unaware of, or injury or illness that is affecting the flow of energy within you. While most blockages can be worked through and overcome with your own awareness and persistence, for persistent blockages getting the assistance of a skilled advisor can help you to resolve these more quickly.

A skilled qigong teacher will be able to quickly identify issues with your movement and posture or even just how you are thinking about things that may take a long time to discover by yourself. They will also be able to help you make adjustments that will allow the energy to flow more freely. These adjustments may be quite substantial, or they could also be very subtle, but you will be able to feel the change in your energy flow when you apply them.

They may even recommend that you seek further assistance or treatment to help remedy injuries or weaknesses in your body that may be impeding your progress. While qigong is a wonderful tool for improving our health and wellbeing, there are many other therapies that can be useful in resolving health issues which will in turn allow your energy to flow more freely. These include dietary changes, herbal remedies, massage, chiropractic adjustment, counselling for psychological distress, and even western medicine and physical therapy. Practicing qigong and learning to feel the flow of energy in your body is valuable in that as well as gently building your health and vitality, it can also help you to uncover and understand sources of blockages to your health and wellbeing that may exist deep within your body and psyche. As you little by little improve the flow of energy through your body, the places where the energy gets stuck become more obvious, and having uncovered them you are in a better position to understand what might be necessary to resolve them.

In my opinion some of the greatest benefits of qigong practice are to be able to take real enjoyment and pleasure in the simple healthy functioning of our bodies. As we practice consistently, little by little we learn to understand ourselves better and better and our practice becomes a tool for self knowledge and discovery. Over time we become more skilful and harmonious in our use of our body and our interaction with the world around us allowing us to be more and more truly 'in the flow'.

Chapter Ten: The Wide World Of Qigong

This may have been the first book you have read about qigong. If so, I hope that you have enjoyed it and found the practices presented in it interesting and useful. At this point you may also be interested to find out more about other qigong practices you may benefit from. Long White Cloud Qigong offers books, dvds, online courses, and other resources for learning a wide range of these practices that you might like to explore.

Below are some of the practices Long White Cloud Qigong has to offer:

Waking the Qi

Because of stress, injury, ill-health, or other factors, your energy can become inactive and withdraw to your centre, going to 'sleep'. This series of practices is designed to wake up and activate your energy to get it flowing through your whole body again. When your flow of energy is healthy and strong and 'awake', not only will your health and vitality increase, but you will be able to sense and work with your energy more easily in whatever you do, including other qigong practices, Taiji (Tai Chi), or other internal energy arts.

Twelve Rivers Qigong

This is a set of twelve qigong exercises that stimulate the organ meridians in the body. These meridians are the same meridians as those used in acupuncture and are like rivers of energy that flow through our bodies. Twelve Rivers Qigong gives us a practical understanding of these meridians and how organ function, posture and emotion affect each other. Practicing Twelve Rivers Qigong activates the meridians, corrects posture, balances emotions and helps to keep our organs healthy and strong.

Between Heaven and Earth

This practice works with the extraordinary meridians in the body. The energy flows in these meridians are powerful like ocean currents.

These meridians relate more to the muscles, connective tissue, bones, and nerves in our bodies. Working with these meridians helps us to understand another layer of our energetic functioning, and when they are fully active allow us to connect more strongly to the energy of heaven and energy of earth.

Qigong Meditation

Qigong Meditation teaches a series of meditations that take you step by step to an amazing place of clarity and stillness. Many people say that these meditations have changed their lives.

Movement in Stillness

Zhan Zhuang or Standing Post is a very powerful type of qigong practice where by standing in stillness externally we find that the energy moves more freely and powerfully inside. Movement in Stillness teaches a selection of these powerful practices and includes instruction on how to get the most out of these practices by avoiding common mistakes.

Qigong Walking

Walking is something that most of us do regularly as part of our daily lives. By walking with qigong awareness you can learn to walk in a way that causes less wear and tear on your body and stimulates your energy flow. Qigong walking teaches a series of walking practices that help you to maintain healthy energy flow and a full and vibrant energy field throughout your day.

Introduction to Qigong Healing

When our own energy is healthy and strong, we are able to use this energy to help others. Introduction to Qigong Healing provides an introduction to using your energy in this way. It is best to have developed a firm foundation in your own qigong practice before exploring this area of qigong application.

Wild Animal Play

Some of the earliest qigong practices involved mimicking the movements of different animals and feeling what these do to the energy of your body. Wild Animal Play teaches movements from Tiger, Snake, Crane, Leopard, and Dragon qigong. These movements are vigorous and great for developing strength, flexibility, balance, agility, power, and fluidity of movement. Underlying theory and relationships to the five elements are also taught for each of these practices.

Release the Power of Your Breath

Breathing is at the centre of qigong, and at the centre of life. Release the Power of Your Breath gives a foundational understanding of the breathing function including anatomy, physiology, chemistry, and psychology. It then applies this understanding to relaxation, alertness, physical performance, and energy awareness.

Further Resources

You can find information about each of these including many free videos on the Long White Cloud Qigong website at
http://www.longwhitecloudqigong.com

About the Author

Throughout his life, John Munro has had an active interest in health and wellbeing. His mother was a naturopath, so throughout his early formative years he was exposed to many different natural methods for improving health and correcting illness. One of these was Qigong, and this combination of working with the mind and the body together to become aware of and direct energy fascinated him.

John went on to formally study many different aspects of health maintenance himself, gaining qualifications in Traditional Chinese Medicine, Neuro Linguistic Programming, Massage, Chinese Reflexology, Personal Training, and of course Qigong. In addition to this he has also studied physics, chemistry and philosophy at a university level. These diverse areas of study all feed into a broad practical understanding of Qigong and an ability to translate important qigong concepts into modern language.

John has previously served as the Secretary and Registrar of *The New Zealand Qigong and Traditional Chinese Medicine Association*, and as Chairperson of *Natural Health Practitioners of New Zealand*. He is also the founder of Long White Cloud Qigong, an international qigong school with students and teachers all over the world, and the author of several popular books on qigong.

Printed in Great Britain
by Amazon